WHITE SHIRTS

DR—To Lin and Joseph, my white shirt guys

BC—For my two sons, Bryant and Kyle

Text © 2006 Deborah Pace Rowley

Illustrations © 2006 Brian Call

DESERET BOOK is a registered trademark of Deseret Book Company.

Visit us at DeseretBook.com

Library of Congress Cataloging-in-Publication Data
Rowley, Deborah Pace.
   White shirts : a baptism keepsake for boys / Deborah Rowley;
illustrated by Brian Call.
       p.   cm.
   ISBN-10 1-59038-633-7 (hardbound : alk. paper)
   ISBN-13 978-1-59038-633-0 (hardbound : alk. paper)
   1. Mormon boys—Religious life—Juvenile literature.   I. Call, Brian D.
II. Title.
   BX8643.C56R69 2006
   242'.632—dc22   2006012730

Printed in China
RR Donnelley
10   9   8   7

White Shirts

By Deborah Pace Rowley

Illustrated by Brian Call

DESERET BOOK

Salt Lake City, Utah

Today you were baptized. I stood in the baptismal font as you came down the stairs into the water. You looked up at me with trusting eyes and flashed that impish grin with missing teeth that always makes me smile.

Suddenly I remembered that day you were blessed as a baby. You were so handsome in your little white shirt and miniature suit. Your grandpa and uncles and I stood around you in a circle. You opened your big eyes, looked up at our hovering faces, and smiled.

That little white shirt reminded me that your spirit had recently stood in the presence of God and that He had saved you to come to earth at this time. I looked at you, so small in our big hands, and thought to myself, *This is Heavenly Father's boy. I am so lucky to be his dad.*

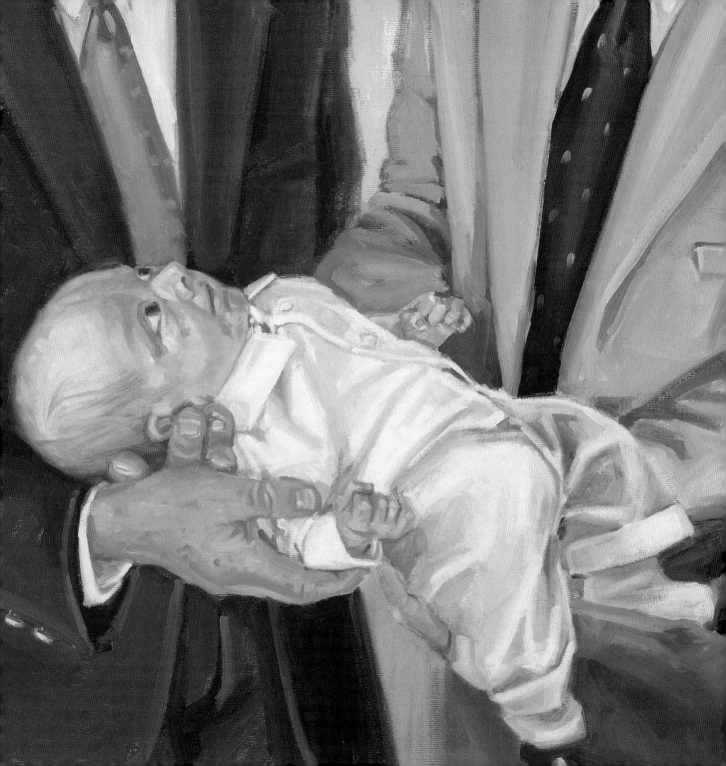

I am still the luckiest dad in the world. Thanks for calling me to the rescue when you climbed too high in the big oak tree. And thanks for telling me the truth about the broken window.

Thanks for coming with me on that fathers and sons' camp-out in the rain and the mud. I think we must have looked like swamp monsters when we came home. Mom made you take two baths in one day to get your body clean after that.

I was so happy you asked me to baptize you. I took your hand and you held my wrist the way we had practiced. Then I said the sacred words of the baptismal prayer and lowered you into the water. Your white shirt represented how clean you were inside, and I knew you could remain that way through repentance and the atonement of Jesus Christ. I hugged you so hard when you came out of the water that your wet shirt soaked mine.

We changed into dry clothes and tried to smooth your hair down in back. Then we walked out of the dressing room, side by side, in our white shirts and ties. I laid my hands on your head and confirmed you a member of The Church of Jesus Christ of Latter-day Saints and conferred upon you the gift of the Holy Ghost.

Remember our lesson on the Holy Ghost in family home evening? I hope that you will learn to recognize those warm, peaceful feelings during family prayer, scripture study, and in your everyday life. I'll show you how important my testimony is to me so you'll want to gain a testimony of your own. I hope Jesus Christ becomes your very best friend.

Anytime you need a father's blessing, I want to be worthy to give you one. I will lay my hands on your head if you are sick or hurt or confused or afraid. You better not jump off the garage and break your leg like I did. But you might need your appendix out just like me. Whatever happens, I'll be there.

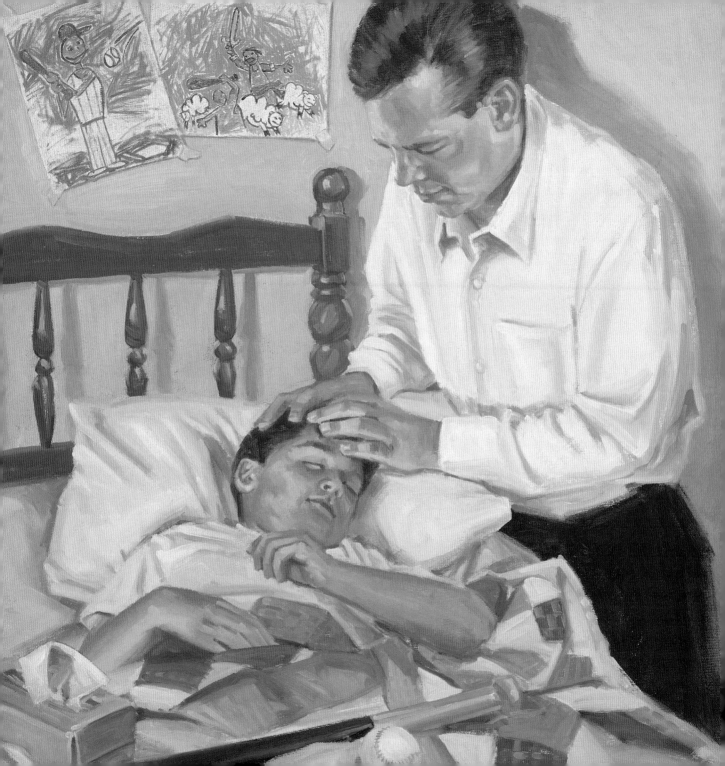

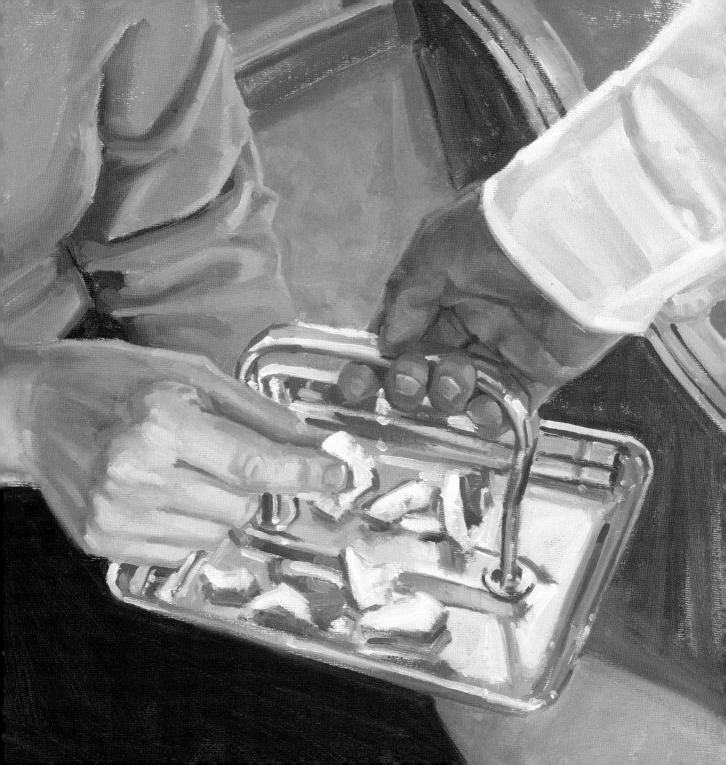

When you are twelve, I will lay my hands on your head again to confer the Aaronic Priesthood upon you and ordain you to the office of a deacon. Mom will be so impressed at the sight of you in your white shirt as you pass her the sacrament each Sunday. Always tuck in your shirttail and remember you have been trusted to hold the priesthood and power of God.

You are growing so tall and strong. Soon you'll be a teenager, and one day you might even beat your dad in basketball. That will be great because I love to watch you win.

To win in life you will need to avoid pornography, keep the Word of Wisdom, and stay morally clean. I want you to know that if you make a mistake and truly repent, the atonement of the Savior can make you clean again.

Before I know it you'll be nineteen. We'll race to the mailbox every day waiting for your mission call. When it comes, you'll rip open the envelope, and I'll jump up and down in the street, shouting, "My son is going on a mission!"

You are going to be an awesome missionary, just like your hero Ammon in the scriptures. For two years, your white shirt and nametag will tell the world that you represent the Church of Jesus Christ. When you return home you'll walk differently off the plane—head and shoulders above the rest. I'll see it immediately and will start to cry. It'll be okay, though, because you'll have to wipe away a tear also.

Mom will be the one crying on the day that you get married. I'm praying that your bride will be as wonderful as mine. In the temple you will wear another white shirt and kneel at the altar across from the girl of your dreams. The two of you will hold hands and listen to the ordinance that will seal you together eternally. That white shirt will remind you that you can become a king, and if you are faithful, you will reign with her by your side forever.

Then, one wonderful day, if we both keep our covenants, I will wait for you in heaven. I will see you return to God with honor, wearing white once again. Everything that we endured on earth will be worth it when we kneel before our Savior, Jesus Christ.

My son, I love you so much. I am so grateful that you made the decision to be baptized. I can't wait for the rest of your life.